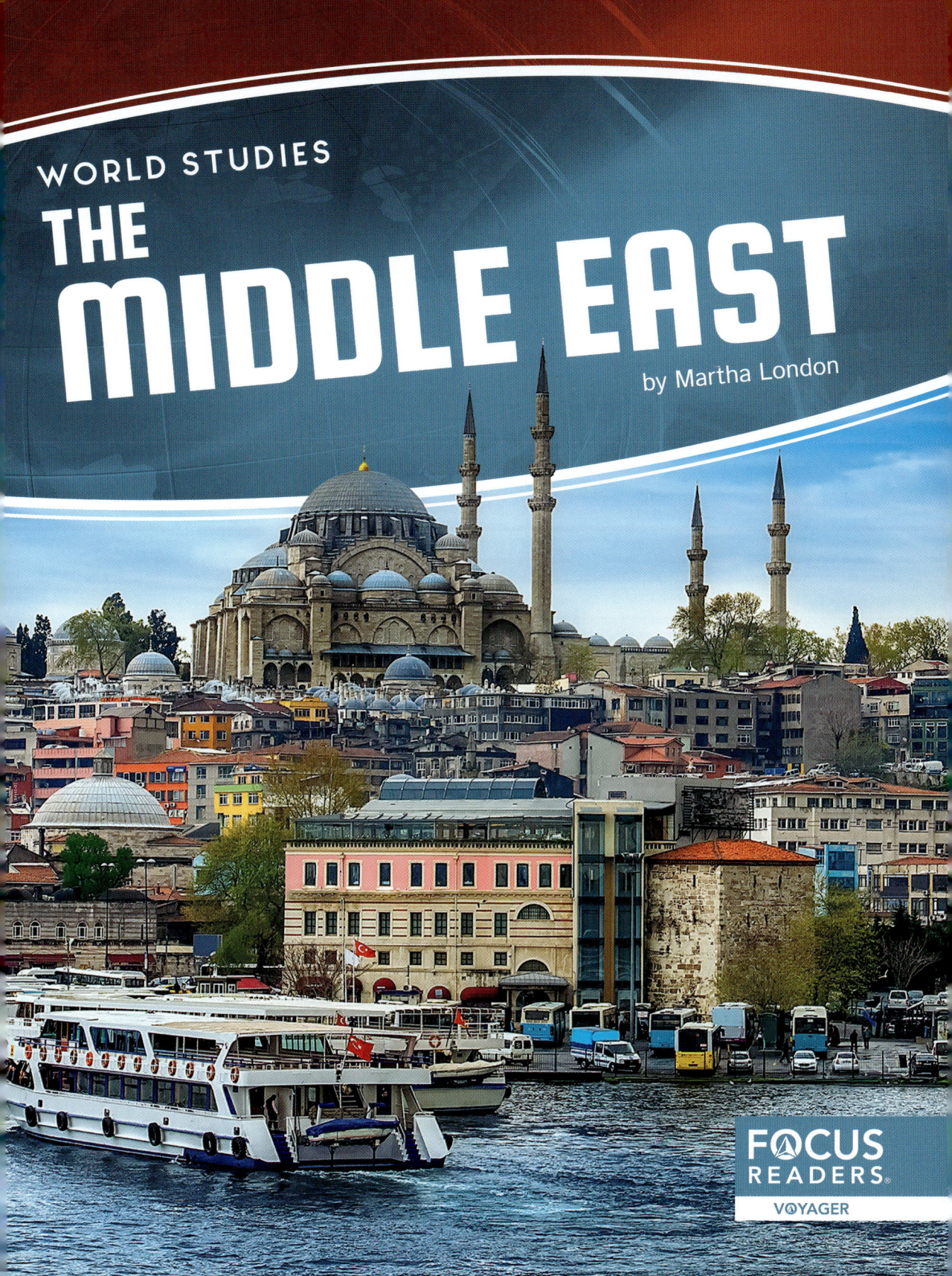

www.focusreaders.com

Copyright © 2021 by Focus Readers®, Lake Elmo, MN 55042. All rights reserved. No part of this book may be reproduced or utilized in any form or by any means without written permission from the publisher.

Focus Readers is distributed by North Star Editions:
sales@northstareditions.com | 888-417-0195

Produced for Focus Readers by Red Line Editorial.

Content Consultant: Angela Joya, PhD, Assistant Professor of International Studies, University of Oregon

Photographs ©: Shutterstock Images, cover, 1, 4–5, 7, 7 (inset), 8–9, 11, 13, 14–15, 17, 20–21, 23, 24, 28–29, 31, 32, 37, 39, 40–41, 43; David Sutherland/Alamy, 19; iStockphoto, 27; Andrew Caballero-Reynolds/AP Images, 34–35; Majdi Fathi/Zuma Press/Newscom, 44

Library of Congress Cataloging-in-Publication Data
Names: London, Martha, author.
Title: The Middle East / Martha London.
Description: Lake Elmo, MN : Focus Readers, [2021] | Series: World studies | Includes index. | Audience: Grades 7-9
Identifiers: LCCN 2020002217 (print) | LCCN 2020002218 (ebook) | ISBN 9781644934005 (hardcover) | ISBN 9781644934760 (paperback) | ISBN 9781644936283 (pdf) | ISBN 9781644935521 (ebook)
Subjects: LCSH: Middle East--Juvenile literature.
Classification: LCC DS44 .L54 2021 (print) | LCC DS44 (ebook) | DDC 956--dc23
LC record available at https://lccn.loc.gov/2020002217
LC ebook record available at https://lccn.loc.gov/2020002218

Printed in the United States of America
Mankato, MN
012021

ABOUT THE AUTHOR
Martha London writes books for young readers. When she isn't writing, you can find her hiking in the woods.

TABLE OF CONTENTS

CHAPTER 1
Welcome to the Middle East 5

CHAPTER 2
History of the Middle East 9

CHAPTER 3
Geography and Climate 15

LANDMARK PROFILE
The Arabian Desert 18

CHAPTER 4
Plants and Animals 21

ANIMAL PROFILE
Green Sawfish 26

CHAPTER 5
Natural Resources and Economy 29

CHAPTER 6
Government and Politics 35

CHAPTER 7
People and Culture 41

Focus on the Middle East • 46
Glossary • 47
To Learn More • 48
Index • 48

CHAPTER 1

WELCOME TO THE MIDDLE EAST

The Middle East exists where Africa, Asia, and Europe meet. Ancient and modern cities bustle along the area's coasts, in deserts, and near mountains. The Middle East is a complex region. The exact boundaries of the Middle East are debated. Many people consider North Africa to be a part of the region. Others include Afghanistan and Pakistan. However, one common definition includes West Asia and the northeast tip of Africa.

The Elburz Mountains rise behind the capital city of Tehran in Iran.

It includes a tiny part of Southeast Europe, too. Turkey is the northernmost country in the Middle East. To its southeast lie Iraq and Iran.

Farther south is the Arabian Peninsula. This area includes Saudi Arabia, Yemen, and the United Arab Emirates (UAE). Qatar, Oman, Kuwait, and Bahrain are also there. This peninsula touches the Red Sea, Persian Gulf, and Arabian Sea.

Jordan lies northwest of the peninsula. Farther northwest is the Mediterranean Sea. Syria, Lebanon, Israel, and the Gaza Strip lie on this sea's coast. Israel and the Gaza Strip touch Egypt. This country is part of Africa. But it has a long history as part of the Middle East.

The region holds some of the world's oldest cities. For example, people have lived in Jerusalem for thousands of years. Istanbul, Turkey, has existed since 700 BCE. It remains a cultural center. The growth of Dubai is more recent. This UAE city is known for its modern architecture.

In many ways, the Middle East is an important part of the global economy. Its diverse peoples play important roles around the world.

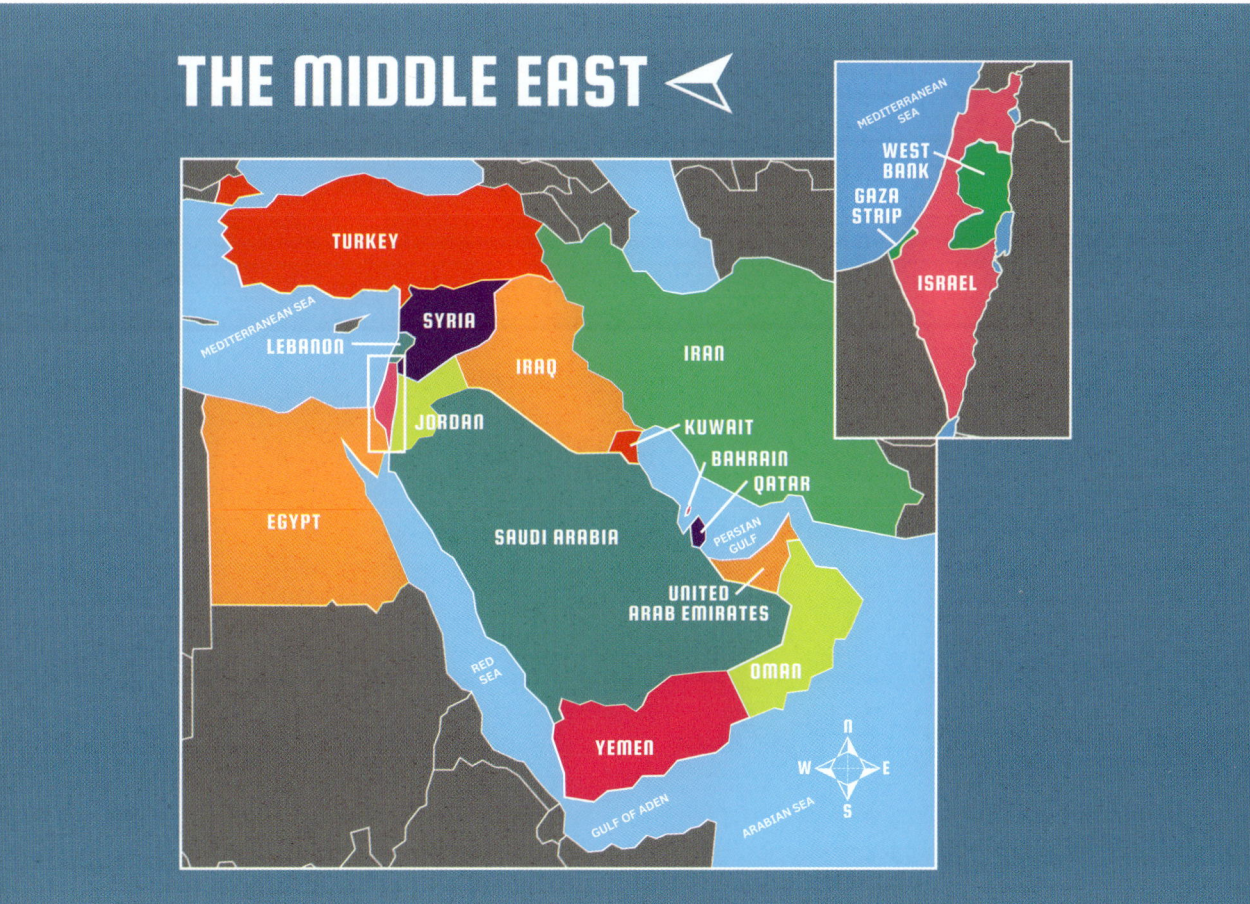

CHAPTER 2

HISTORY OF THE MIDDLE EAST

Humans have lived in the Middle East for more than 100,000 years. Early humans moved from place to place in small groups. Approximately 11,000 years ago, however, people began farming in an area known as Mesopotamia. This area stretches from the southeastern edge of present-day Turkey through Syria and Iraq.

People moved less when they had farms. Over time, some people formed complex communities.

In ancient Mesopotamia, people created massive buildings known as ziggurats. This ruin was in the city of Ur, located in present-day Iraq.

For example, Sumer formed in approximately 4000 BCE. Sumerians developed one of the world's first written languages.

Ancient Egypt was another major **civilization**. It formed around 3000 BCE. For thousands of years, ancient Egypt was the region's most powerful civilization. Its people produced many achievements, such as the Pyramids of Giza.

Other empires rose and fell. Trade began to wrap around the Mediterranean Sea. This trade connected the Middle East more to southern Europe and northern Africa. In addition, Judaism developed on the eastern Mediterranean coast.

In the 500s BCE, the Persian Empire rose to power in what is now Iran. It took over many parts of the Middle East, including Turkey and Egypt. By 100 CE, however, the Roman Empire had taken over much of this land. Christianity had

Mesopotamians used wedge-shaped writing known as cuneiform.

formed as well. In fact, the Romans helped spread Christianity throughout much of the Middle East.

In 610 CE, Islam formed in present-day Saudi Arabia. A number of Arab tribes united under this religion. They spread. By 750, they controlled the entire region except Turkey. They also ruled much of North Africa, Spain, and Portugal. This empire was called the Caliphate. It lasted in some form for more than 600 years. People practiced many branches of Islam, Christianity, Judaism, and other religions throughout the empire.

Under the Caliphate, the Middle East became more connected with other parts of the world. Arabic and Spanish cultures, languages, and foods mixed with one another. Traders from Asia brought new information. Paper, for instance, came from China. Scientists advanced their knowledge of math and medicine. The Middle East developed more than Europe during this period.

In the 1200s, the Mongol Empire took power. Then, a deadly plague swept through in the 1300s. Next, Turkic groups united. Between 1453 and 1566, the Ottoman Empire conquered most of the region. It took over parts of Europe, too. The empire started to decline in the 1700s. Finally, it fell after World War I (1914–1918). Allied forces split the Ottoman Empire into territories.

The United Kingdom and France **colonized** several areas in the region. After World War II

(1939–1945), the Middle East changed again. Israel formed in 1948. Many countries gained independence. But outside nations still tried to control the region. And Middle Eastern countries faced conflicts within and across their borders.

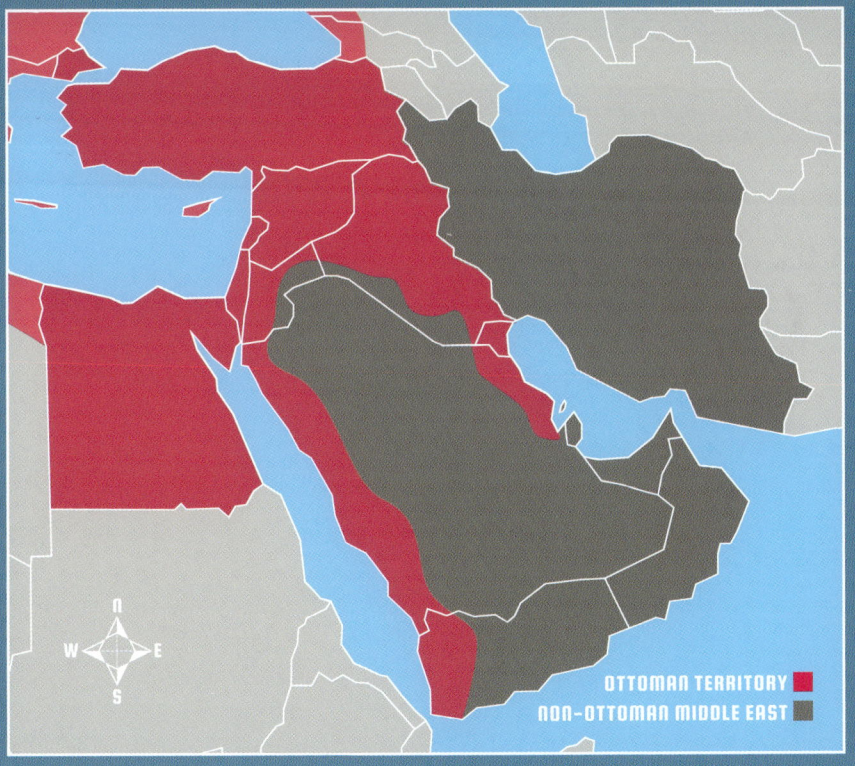

CHAPTER 3

GEOGRAPHY AND CLIMATE

The Middle East has many different geographies and climates. Turkey, Iraq, and Iran all feature mountain ranges. These areas tend to experience cold winters. Some receive large amounts of rain and snow. But parts of these countries also have steppe climates. Few trees grow there.

At the same time, southern Turkey lies on the Mediterranean Sea. This part of Turkey is warmer and wetter than the country's mountain regions.

A steppe is a dry, grassy area.

Other areas along the Mediterranean have similar climates. Israel and Lebanon lie near this sea. Western Jordan and Syria do as well.

The Arabian Peninsula lies to the south. Saudi Arabia, Oman, and Yemen are the largest countries on this peninsula. The area also includes Bahrain, Qatar, Kuwait, and the UAE. Much of the peninsula is a desert. It is hot and dry. Summer temperatures can reach 129 degrees Fahrenheit (54°C). However, some of the coasts experience wetter climates. Together, inland mountains and seas can create rainy conditions. In fact, parts of Yemen are tropical.

Several rivers also run through the Middle East. The Nile River flows through Egypt. Meanwhile, the Tigris and Euphrates flow through Turkey, Syria, and Iraq. These two rivers join together in Iraq. They form a river called the Shatt al-Arab.

▲ The Tigris River provides irrigation as it flows through Iraq.

Climate change is affecting all regions of the world. The Middle East is especially at risk in this crisis. For example, sea levels in the Mediterranean are rising. This change hurts coastal towns. In addition, many areas are experiencing warmer temperatures and lower rainfall. These changes reduce the amount of fresh water available to people.

LANDMARK PROFILE

THE ARABIAN DESERT

The Arabian Desert is the second-largest desert in the world. It covers 900,000 square miles (2.3 million sq km). The desert covers parts of Yemen and Oman in the south. It spreads through Saudi Arabia, the UAE, Qatar, and Kuwait. In the north, the desert covers parts of Jordan and Iraq.

The Empty Quarter lies in the southeastern part of the Arabian Desert. As little as 1.2 inches (3.0 cm) of rain falls in the Empty Quarter each year. The Empty Quarter is also the largest sand-only area on Earth. Massive sand dunes cover the landscape. The dunes can reach heights of more than 800 feet (240 m).

Few people live permanently in the Empty Quarter. But some travel through it. Bedouin peoples have lived in and traveled through the Empty Quarter for generations. Bedouin peoples

▲ Bedouin peoples have traditionally lived in a series of temporary camps.

are **nomadic**. They are experts of the desert. They know where water sources are.

The Arabian Desert can seem hostile. Strong winds make it hard to see. Water sources are limited. But the Arabian Desert is full of plant and animal life that make use of the scarce water supplies. Most species in this area can go for long periods with limited water.

CHAPTER 4

PLANTS AND ANIMALS

Plants and animals in the Middle East have all adapted to where they live. For example, the Mediterranean area receives enough rainfall for fruit trees to grow. Olive and fig trees are common in the Mediterranean. At the same time, the date palm can grow in the desert. This fruit tree is important throughout the Middle East.

Ghaf trees are native to the Arabian Desert. They need much less water than most other trees.

Camels and ghaf trees have both adapted to survive in places with little water.

A ghaf tree's roots sink deep into the ground. They find water that most plants cannot reach.

Some desert plants bloom quickly. Their seeds have a coating that stops them from growing. The rain washes off the coating. When that happens, the seeds grow rapidly. In this way, these plants wait for the right time to start growing. After a rainstorm, a desert completely changes.

Desert animals have also adapted to their environment. The Arabian spiny-tailed lizard is common in the Arabian Desert. This reptile digs holes in the sand and stays in them. In this way, the lizard avoids the hot sun. It can stay cool enough even in summer.

Wild goats live in the mountains of Iran. Their hooves help them climb the rocky mountains. Turkey is also home to mountain life. Hardy trees such as pines and firs grow on mountain slopes.

⚠ The Arabian spiny-tailed lizard uses its sharp tail to defend against predators.

Oak and maple trees grow closer to the base of the mountains. The trees are able to survive in the drier mountain climate. They can also handle changes in temperatures from summer to winter.

In addition, a variety of birds fly throughout the Middle East. Ibis, gulls, and diving birds such as grebes live along the coasts. Falcons, hawks, and eagles can also be found in the region. People often use falcons to hunt.

▲ A jerboa's long hind legs help it hop rapidly across the sand.

Weasels and rodents are also common in the Middle East. The jerboa is a rodent that lives in the desert. This animal has long legs and feet. It can leap more than 10 feet (3.0 m) to escape danger. A jerboa might never drink water in its life.

Instead, the animal gets water from the plants and insects it eats.

Ocean life is also important to the Middle East. For example, the Red Sea is located along the western coast of the Arabian Peninsula. The Red Sea holds several coral reefs. Many species of animals make their home in reefs. Clown fish, eels, and stingrays all live near reefs in the Red Sea.

The Middle East is home to many plants and animals. Some are found nowhere else in the world. Each is specially equipped to live in its habitat.

THINK ABOUT IT

What plants and animals are common where you live? How have they adapted to their environment?

ANIMAL PROFILE

GREEN SAWFISH

Green sawfish live in the Persian Gulf and the Red Sea. They are a type of ray. These rays have long snouts. Sharp teeth line their saw-like snouts. For this reason, sawfish are sometimes called carpenter sharks.

Green sawfish are one of the largest species of sawfish in the world. They can grow to be more than 23 feet (7.0 m) long. These fish can take 10 years to become adults. They live up to 50 years in the wild.

A green sawfish uses its snout to kill prey. It slashes its head back and forth quickly. The ray's teeth cut the prey. A sawfish's mouth lies on the bottom of its head. Sometimes, a sawfish uses its snout to bring prey to the seafloor. Then the sawfish eats.

People do not hunt sawfish. Even so, fishing crews still catch them by accident. Sometimes,

▲ Green sawfish typically swim in shallow water near coasts.

the animals' long snouts get tangled in fishing nets. Some parts of sawfish have value. So, fishers often kill any sawfish caught in their nets. For this reason, the number of green sawfish has been falling. They are endangered. But many people are trying to save them.

CHAPTER 5

NATURAL RESOURCES AND ECONOMY

Many Middle Eastern countries rely on exports to support their economies. Exports are goods sold to other countries. For example, Middle Eastern countries sell more than 40 percent of the world's dates. Many export olive oil, too. Turkey also sells clothing and car products to other countries. And Israel buys raw diamonds from other countries. Then it sells polished diamonds around the world.

In some parts of the Middle East, people have grown olives for thousands of years.

However, the region's largest exports are oil, petroleum, and natural gas. These fossil fuels provide energy in a number of ways. Oil and petroleum often fuel vehicles. Natural gas is often used to heat homes.

For these reasons, fossil fuels are in high demand around the world. The Middle East holds much of the world's oil supply. As a result, many large countries, including China and the United States, depend on fossil fuels from the Middle East. Several Middle Eastern countries depend mostly on fossil fuel exports for their wealth. Some of these countries are Saudi Arabia, Oman, Qatar, and Kuwait.

However, countries in the region cannot depend on fossil fuels forever. Oil takes millions of years to form. It is a limited resource. Burning fossil fuels is also one of the largest contributors to

▲ At petrochemical plants, petroleum is refined to produce plastics and many other products.

climate change. For reasons such as these, some countries are changing their economies. Saudi Arabia, for example, has increased its focus on education, tourism, and health.

Middle Eastern economies struggle over access to fresh water. Egypt is one of the region's few countries with easy access to this resource. Some countries do not have large supplies of fresh water. Others have important underground sources of water that they must use carefully.

▲ The Ermenek dam in Turkey is also a hydropower plant. It uses the flow of water to produce electricity.

Some countries also rely on rivers that flow into their countries. However, other countries may build dams on certain rivers. A dam blocks a river's water. It helps control flooding. A dam also creates a lake-like supply of water. This supply can help provide water for farms.

At the same time, a dam reduces how much water a river carries downstream. For this reason, dams have created problems for certain countries in the Middle East. For instance, Turkey has built many dams on the Tigris and Euphrates Rivers. Those rivers flow south through Syria and Iraq. As a result, Syria and Iraq receive much less water downstream.

Some countries rely on rain for their crops. For this reason, droughts are a leading cause of food shortages. Between 1998 and 2012, a severe drought hit the western Middle East. Experts believe it was the area's worst drought in 900 years. And as climate change progresses, droughts will become worse and more common.

THINK ABOUT IT

Rivers are natural resources that flow across borders. How should countries share resources such as water?

CHAPTER 6

GOVERNMENT AND POLITICS

Several kinds of governments exist in the Middle East. For example, Jordan, Qatar, and Saudi Arabia have monarchies. One family has ruled Saudi Arabia since the country formed in 1932. The family controls all parts of government.

Iran used to have a monarchy. But in 1979, a revolution overthrew that government. Since then, a religious leader runs much of Iran. This ruler serves for life. But Iran also has a president.

Qaboos bin Said was Oman's sultan, or monarch, from 1970 until his death in 2020.

Citizens elect this leader. The president controls some parts of government.

The UAE's government works differently. The UAE is made up of seven states, known as emirates. Each emirate is ruled by a leader from one of its tribes. These seven leaders work together in a **federation**.

Israel's government is democratic. But instead of voting for candidates, citizens vote for political parties. Then party members become part of the Knesset. This body makes laws for the country. Israel's prime minister often comes from the party that receives the most votes. But that party may have to work with other parties to form a majority.

At the same time, Israel occupies the West Bank and Gaza Strip. The population of these two territories is mostly Palestinian. The West Bank has its own government. But it has limited control.

▲ The Israeli government has built large walls and fences to separate Israel from the West Bank and Gaza Strip.

Israel controls much of the area's planning, construction, and law enforcement. Israel controls Gaza even more. It also blocks most goods and people from coming into and out of Gaza.

Many people are struggling for better governments. In 2011, people across the Middle East and North Africa overthrew their leaders. The events began in the North African country of Tunisia. They were known as the Arab uprisings.

In Egypt, citizens overthrew a 30-year **dictatorship**. They wanted control over their government. They demanded social justice, freedom, and dignity. In 2012, Egyptians voted in a new government. However, Egypt's army took over in 2013. Many Egyptians continue to struggle to pay for food and housing.

People in Yemen and Syria also took part in the Arab uprisings. Yemeni people kicked out a leader who had ruled for 30 years. Saudi Arabia tried to influence Yemen's new government. The UAE did as well. But Yemeni people wanted control over their own country. As a result, a war began in 2014. The war has devastated the civilians of Yemen. Tens of thousands of people have been killed. Millions face starvation.

Syria's leader held on to power during the Arab uprisings. But a civil war broke out in 2012. As of

▲ Tawakkol Karman won the Nobel Peace Prize in 2011 for her work leading human rights protests in Yemen.

2020, the war continued. Hundreds of thousands have died. Millions have fled their homes.

Foreign governments have also caused conflict in the region. For example, US forces invaded Iraq in 2003. They overthrew Iraq's leader. They fought a war there until 2011. As of 2020, Iraq was still struggling to form a stable government. The reasons are complex. But many experts believe the US war is one major reason.

CHAPTER 7

PEOPLE AND CULTURE

The Middle East is home to many ethnic and cultural groups. For example, Kurdish people are native to the region. Many Kurds live in the mountains of Turkey, Syria, Iraq, and Iran. They do not have their own country. But they have a distinct culture and language. Kurds face **discrimination** and violence across the region.

Arab peoples are one of the region's largest groups. The Arabic language joins them together.

The kolobal is a traditional Kurdish jacket made from felt, worn in the Howraman Valley in Iran.

But people speak different kinds of Arabic. And there are many other differences among Arab peoples. In fact, some experts believe Arab may not be a helpful label.

Religion in the Middle East is also complex. Many people practice Islam. But there are different **sects** of Islam. Sunni and Shia are two main sects. Most Muslims in the Middle East are Sunni. But Shia Muslims are majorities in countries such as Iraq and Iran. There is also diversity within Muslim sects. In Saudi Arabia, people follow several kinds of Sunni Islam. In Iran, Shia traditions mix with Persian culture.

Iran is home to other faiths, such as Baha'i, Christianity, and Judaism. Baha'i was formed in Iran in the 1860s. One common belief of Baha'is is to accept all other religions. Zoroastrianism also began in Iran. This ancient religion continues

▲ Turkey's Hagia Sophia has served as a church, a mosque, and a museum during its long history.

to shape Iran's culture. One of the religion's festivals is Nowruz, or the Persian New Year. Nowruz remains a major celebration in Iran.

In Israel, most people are Jewish. At the same time, a large number of Israeli Jews are not religious. They are culturally Jewish. But they may not believe in God.

Rich arts traditions exist across the region as well. Some artists still practice ancient traditions.

▲ Young Palestinians practice break dancing, a type of hip-hop dancing.

For example, some Turkish artists still practice an art known as ebru. These artists paint colorful patterns on water. Then they place paper on the water, and the patterns go onto the paper.

Other artists practice newer traditions. For example, Palestine features a thriving hip-hop scene. Egypt also has many kinds of music, including mahragan. This music often mixes electronic beats with traditional Egyptian music.

In addition, movements of people have had huge effects across the region. Between 2005 and 2015, millions of people moved to the Middle East for economic opportunity. Most of these people moved to Saudi Arabia, the UAE, and Kuwait.

At the same time, even more **migrants** left their homes because of crises. For example, millions of Palestinian **refugees** live in Jordan, Lebanon, and Syria. But most migrants still live in their home country. They fled to a different area in that country. The peoples and cultures in the Middle East are always changing.

THINK ABOUT IT

Artists in the Middle East practice ancient and new traditions. What art forms are practiced where you live?

FOCUS ON
THE MIDDLE EAST

Write your answers on a separate piece of paper.

1. Write a paragraph describing the main ideas of Chapter 5.

2. Water is scarce in some Middle Eastern countries. What natural resources are scarce where you live? How can people conserve them?

3. When was the Ottoman Empire split into separate territories?
    - A. after the fall of the Roman Empire
    - B. after World War I
    - C. after World War II

4. Why did farms enable people to live in one place as a large group?
    - A. Farms made people lazy and not interested in moving around.
    - B. Farms provided people with a large, dependable supply of food.
    - C. Farming proved to be more fun than hunting for food.

Answer key on page 48.

GLOSSARY

civilization
A large group of people with a shared history and culture.

climate change
A human-caused global crisis involving long-term changes in Earth's temperature and weather patterns.

colonized
Established control over an area and the people who live there.

dictatorship
A form of government in which one leader has absolute power.

discrimination
Unfair treatment of others based on who they are or how they look.

federation
A collection of territories that are largely independent but have a central government.

migrants
People who attempt to permanently move far from their home, often but not always to a new country.

nomadic
Having no set home but traveling from place to place, often with the seasons, to find food.

refugees
People forced to leave their homes due to war or other dangers.

sects
Branches of a religion distinct from other branches.

TO LEARN MORE

BOOKS

Capek, Michael. *The Syrian Conflict*. Minneapolis: Abdo Publishing, 2017.

Randolph, Joanne, ed. *Living and Working in Ancient Mesopotamia*. New York: Enslow Publishing, 2018.

Robinson, Anthony, and Annemarie Young. *Young Palestinians Speak: Living Under Occupation*. Northampton, MA: Interlink, 2017.

NOTE TO EDUCATORS

Visit **www.focusreaders.com** to find lesson plans, activities, links, and other resources related to this title.

INDEX

Bahrain, 6–7, 16

Egypt, 6–7, 10, 16, 31, 38, 44–45

Iran, 6–7, 10, 15, 22, 35, 41–43

Iraq, 6–7, 9, 15–16, 18, 33, 39, 41–42

Israel, 6–7, 13, 16, 29, 36–37, 43

Jordan, 6–7, 16, 18, 35, 45

Kuwait, 6–7, 16, 18, 30, 45

Lebanon, 6–7, 16, 45

North Africa, 5, 11, 37

Oman, 6–7, 16, 18, 30

Palestine, 36, 44–45

Qatar, 6–7, 16, 18, 30, 35

Saudi Arabia, 6–7, 11, 16, 18, 30–31, 35, 38, 42, 45

Syria, 6–7, 9, 16, 33, 38, 41, 45

Turkey, 6–7, 9–11, 15–16, 22, 29, 33, 41

United Arab Emirates (UAE), 6–7, 16, 18, 36, 38, 45

Yemen, 6–7, 16, 18, 38

Answer Key: 1. Answers will vary; 2. Answers will vary; 3. B; 4. B

Children's 956 LON
London, Martha
The Middle East

05/27/22